KIDS PRAYER SERIES

KIDS PRAYER SERIES

Paperback ISBN: 978-1-965593-49-3

Published by:
Cornerstone Publishing

A Division of Cornerstone Creativity Group LLC
Info@thecornerstonepublishers.com
www.thecornerstonepublishers.com

Author's Contact:
simi.olushola@gmail.com

DEDICATION

To my mother, Deaconess Bamidele Hannah Abeke Oyebanjo.

My first Bible and Sunday School teacher. Thank you for teaching my young mind about Jesus; this still remains the best legacy. I love you now and always.

-Similoluwa (Ayarabiasa, fondly called by you)

Contents

1

APPRECIATION

It was a beautiful rainy evening and David wanted to ride his bicycle so desperately. All week, he had been telling Mrs. Fash how he would ride his bicycle on Saturday evening, but it had rained all morning and David could not go out as planned. Now, his dad was out with his mom; his brother Elijah had gone out for sports, while his sister was busy in the kitchen making waffles for herself. He knew his only hope was Isaiah. David went to his big brother, Isaiah, who was busy on his laptop in his room.

"Hello, big brother Isaiah," David started. Isaiah smiled knowingly.

"Hmm, when I hear 'big brother Isaiah', I know you have a request. Go ahead and ask for up to half of my kingdom." Isaiah and David laughed, knowing Isaiah had borrowed the expression from the Scriptures. David hugged his big brother and Isaiah said, "Okay, I know you have a request. What is it and stop all this *mushy mushy*," referring to the hug and smiles David was throwing at him. He knew his little brother, who had just turned seven was pretty smart at making his requests undeniable.

"I want to ride my bicycle outside and there's no one to watch me. Elijah has left for his track meet." David said, searching his brother's face.

"But it rained, and the ground is wet, David," Isaiah told him, hoping David would change his mind so he could continue what he was doing on the laptop. He was actually sending an email. David went to the window to check again but was surprised by the beautiful bow he saw in the sky. He was thrilled to see the rainbow.

"I see the rainbow! I see the rainbow!" David yelled excitedly.

Isaiah got up and joined David at the window.

"Yes, David. Do you know the meaning of the rainbow?" Isaiah asked his excited little brother.

"Our Sunday school teacher taught us it's God's promise never to wipe out mankind with water again."

"Yes, David, and generations have passed, and God has been faithful to His promise and His Word. He made a covenant with man never to destroy the world with a flood again."

"What does covenant mean?" David appeared confused.

"Covenant means a promise; that's the best way I can explain it for now."

"But what about the floods and hurricanes that occur and kill people?"

"True, David, they are called natural disasters, but there has never been a flood that happened worldwide all at once and killed everyone or wiped out every living creature. So God has kept His promise, and the rainbow reminds us after it rains that God is faithful."

"I love the colors of the rainbow. I'm happy it means God has a covenant with man never to wipe us out with a flood anymore."

"Yes, David. It's important for you to know and learn Bible stories and understand what God tells us in His Word. Now, let's go and have a ride."

"Yesss!!!" David was excited. "Thank you, Isaiah, for your time. I'm also thankful to God for being so kind to us and not letting any flood take us away."

Isaiah laughed at his brother's little prayer of appreciation. "Correct, David. We need to show our appreciation to God for keeping His covenant and promise." He clasped his hands for prayer, and David joined him. "Lord, we are so thankful for all the wonders You created—the sun, the moon, the solar system, the sky, the rainbow, the wind, and everything. We appreciate Your handiwork, and as little David rides his bicycle, we trust there will be no more rain to stop him from having fun this evening."

David smiled but said the "Amen" seriously and loudly. Isaiah smiled at the way he ended his prayer; it sounded funny, but he tried to show his little brother he cared about his playtime.

"Thank you, Isaiah," David offered again as they both left Isaiah's room upstairs. David felt happy to be reminded of the meaning of the rainbow and for God keeping His part of the deal never to destroy the earth with water again. David was full of appreciation in his heart.

Reflection

Appreciation is the bedrock of more blessings. Jesus gave thanks when He was breaking bread, and it multiplied (Luke 9:16). For the favors you need, be thankful; for the ones you have received, be thankful; for the creations of God and wonders of His might, be thankful; for time to play games and ride bicycles, be thankful too.

"Oh, give thanks to the Lord, for He is good! For His mercy endures forever." (Psalm 107:1).

2

TALENTS AND SKILLS

It was Elijah's 13th birthday—he was officially a teenager! Kiki wanted to give her brother a special gift but was unsure what to choose. She loved all her brothers dearly and wanted to make sure this gift was perfect. Then it came to her—Elijah loved the color red. She asked her mum to get her a big red cardboard from the store, and with it, she made a beautiful birthday card. Inside, she wrote:

Roses are red

The sky is blue

You are 13 today

You are a teenager

Love you, Big Brother

Happy Birthday, Elijah!

Love, Kiki

Elijah had just returned from school and immediately noticed the red card on his bed. He smiled, guessing who had made the gift. Although he was tired from school, he was excited it was his birthday and knew his family had something special planned, even though he wasn't sure what. Dropping his bag, he picked up the card, and his face lit up with joy.

"Kiki, where are you? I love my card!" he called out.

Kiki came out of her room, smiling and happy for her brother.

"I love my birthday card! I didn't know you could make something like this. It's beautiful!"

"I didn't know I could, either," Kiki replied, blushing. "I just tried."

"You're very talented," Elijah observed. "I also remember you making some craftwork for Mom the other day."

"What does 'talented' mean?" David, who had just entered the living room, asked.

Elijah smiled at his younger brother and replied, "Being talented means you have a natural ability to do something. It could be singing, drawing, or..."

"Painting!" David interjected, excited that he understood the meaning of 'talented.'

"Yes, David," Kiki affirmed.

"So, does it mean Mum is talented at making fried rice or chicken Alfredo?" David asked, and Elijah laughed.

"No, Mum is good at cooking because it's a skill she learned. Talent is a God-given ability."

"I love this explanation, Elijah," Kiki remarked. "It makes it clearer. Our Sunday school teacher taught us about talents and skills just last month."

David seemed satisfied with the explanation. "So, Dad is talented at preaching since he does it every Sunday."

"I think so," Elijah said. "Because that's something you can only do with the Spirit of God."

"Happy Birthday, Elijah," David said, hugging his brother. He then added, "Mum said she's bringing in your cake soon."

"Shhh...," Kiki said to her younger brother, putting a finger to her lips.

"Oops! It was supposed to be a secret," David said, covering his mouth and looking sheepishly at his brother.

"It's okay, David," Elijah assured him. "I know Mum always plans

something special for our birthdays."

He then turned to Kiki and said, "Thank you, Kiki. I pray that you draw so well and make beautiful cards that will sell nationwide."

Kiki's smile broadened. "Amen," she said.

Elijah continued, "I also pray for everyone in the family, that God will continue to bless our talents and skills so we can continue to be exceptional. May we use our talents and skills to honor God and bless mankind, in Jesus' name."

"Amen," Kiki and David chorused.

Reflection

Your gifts and talents can profit you greatly. They can take you to places you never imagined, but never let pride get in the way. Always give glory to God as Joseph did, and never toy with or trade your talents for pleasure as Samson did.

"Every good gift and every perfect gift is from above, and comes down from the Father of lights, with whom there is no variation or shadow of turning." (James 1:17)

3

FIRE OUTBREAK

The phone alarm system went off and both Mr. and Mrs. Fash received an alert that there was a fire outbreak at Isaiah and Elijah's high school. Immediately, they made several attempts to call the school, but the calls did not go through. A general message was later sent to assure the parents that the fire department had come on time and the fire had been quickly stopped with very little damage, and no injury or loss of life occurred.

Mr. Fash picked up his first two sons after he had picked Kiki and David. David listened to the conversation of his dad and brothers and learned of the fire outbreak.

"There was a fire in your school?" David asked, wide-eyed.

"Yes," Isaiah answered.

"Did anybody die?" David was scared now

Isaiah looked at his brother with surprise. "David! Why would you think of anyone dying? No one died, thank God!"

"Were you injured, did you run from the fire?" David probed again.

"Yes, we had to be escorted to a large hall," Elijah answered. "I met Isaiah on the hallway. Nothing bad happened to any student or staff. The firefighters came on time. I think it happened in the laboratory but was quickly stopped."

"I like firefighters," Kiki gushed. "They are always on time."

"Yes they do an excellent job," Isaiah affirmed. "But sometimes they can't help it if the fire had gone bad before their arrival."

"Yes, and those times are difficult times for them, but let's thank God your school had such timely interventions," Mr. Fash remarked. "They sent a text message to your mom and I, and we called but it did not go through. But we got another text that the fire was under control."

"Anytime I hear of a fire, my mind kind of remember the cities that God destroyed with fire in the Bible," Kiki stated, recalling her Bible stories.

"You mean *So-dam* and...?" David tried recalling the exact names but couldn't. "Mom taught us last year in our morning devotions."

"Sodom and Gomorrah," Isaiah offered.

"And they got destroyed because they kept sinning against God and wouldn't repent," Mr. Fash concluded.

"Was that what happened in Isaiah and Elijah's school today, Dad?" David asked.

"Oh, no, David! God is not angry with the school," Kiki answered.

"No David," Mr. Fash answered. "This was a kind of accident. They texted that there was a fire outbreak in the laboratory, and we are thankful to God for putting a stop to it; no one died or got injured."

"Dad, I pray all our schools will never catch fire, in Jesus' name," David said, with his hands clasped.

"Amen," everyone said.

Kiki also prayed: "May God protect us from all forms of fire outbreak. May the Lord protect us, our loved ones and our properties too, in Jesus' name." And everyone said, "Amen".

Reflection

Be careful with things that can cause a fire. Not all fires come from God; some are out of negligence, and we will be accountable for such. So, let's be careful.

He who dwells in the secret place of the Most High Shall abide under the shadow of the Almighty. I will say of the Lord, "He is my refuge and my fortress; My God, in Him I will trust." (Psalm 91:1-2)

4

THE CHURCH

"I love Sundays!" Kiki stated to her friend, Nora, on the phone. It was Saturday evening and Nora, who attended another church, was feeling reluctant to be in church the next morning. Kiki, on the other hand, was looking forward to the Sunday service in her church.

"I love to sleep extra in the morning," Nora said.

"But you slept extra on Saturday morning," Kiki retorted with a chuckle.

"I know," Nora admitted.

"In our church, we have different departments and do lots of fun and exciting things. We have our online zoom meetings and practice for different presentations. We have our "Code" days, in which we wear certain colors - CODE RED, for example - and the colors always stand for something. We have rewards, journal reading and snacks at the end of each service."

"That's so *wow!*" Nora said, emphasizing on the 'wow'

"We also have Bible competitions and the like," Kiki continued. "And the best part for me are our presentations on special days like Christmas, Easter, Mother's Days, Father's Day, Thanksgiving, and so on."

"Can you invite me over to your church?" Nora pleaded, her eyes widening with excitement.

"We have our "Friends Sunday" and so on. You are free to come at any Sunday service, though. I will also invite you to meet my other church friends," Kiki replied.

"I would love to meet your friends," Nora stated.

"The most important thing is that I invite you to the house of Jesus, where He will be your friend. He loves children a lot and will want you to come over," Kiki responded

"How do you know that Jesus loves children," Nora asked, getting more interested in the conversation.

"Because He says it in His word, the Bible. He says we belong to His kingdom. I think it's in Matthew 19:14 - yes, it is! *'But Jesus said, "Let the little children come to Me, and do not forbid them; for of such is the kingdom of heaven"'* Kiki explained.

I guess it is because we are innocent, and He loves us that way," Nora stated.

"I think it's more because we can be molded. According to my mom, a kid's mind is simple and trusting; that is why God wants adults

to be like us, to get to heaven. He says, 'Assuredly, I say to you, unless *you are converted and become as little children, you will by no means enter the kingdom of heaven.* (Matthew 18:3, KJV)'"

Nora was super impressed now. "I am going to come to your church," she said. "I will let my dad and mom know and I'll come. I will start to attend more of our church services too."

"God gave us churches, so we can have our own community too," Kiki explained further. "Just like the way we have TikTok and Instagram online communities, the church community is for friends and family. I love our church!"

"I can see you do!" Nora chipped in. "Do you also pray for your church, knowing you and the way you like to pray?" Nora asked.

"Yes, I do pray for our church. We do that every day, with Dad and Mom. We pray for God to heal the sick, provide for the needy, and forgive all our sins. We pray for increase in all areas. We pray for the children, the men and the women. We pray for the pastor and other ministers, as well as the workers. We pray for the different countries of the world. We pray for our leaders. Most importantly, we pray for the body of Christ – that is, all the churches of Christ – worldwide. Yes, we pray, Nora."

"Hmm..I bet you do!" Nora replied. "I think we should pray together for the body of Christ now."

"Sure," said Kiki. "May God bless the body of Christ to keep standing in the light of Christ - strong, powerful and unmoved in Jesus' name."

"Amen." The girls chorused on both ends.

Reflection

The joy of going to church is to know the Lord the more. God does not want us to forsake our services and togetherness. When last did you go to church? Ensure to be there this Sunday!

"I was glad when they said to me, let us go into the house of the Lord." (Psalm 122:1)

5

DRUG ABUSE

David noticed some medications in a bag beside Grandma's table. Surprised at the number of medications he saw, he went to Kiki and called her out of her room.

"Kiki, come quick, I need to show you something!"

Alarmed at the urgency, Kiki got up from her bed and went to

David, who was standing at the entrance. "What is it, David?"

"I think Grandma is on drugs! We need to let Dad and Mom know quickly!"

Kiki got more confused. "How did you know? What did you see?"

David pulled Kiki to Grandma's room and they saw the medications she had recently received from the neighboring BHS pharmacy. Kiki smiled at her six-year-old brother's reasoning.

"David," she started, "these are Grandma's medications from BHS pharmacy. She is not on drugs like you mean it, but she is taking the medications her doctor prescribed for her."

"Well, my teacher says drugs are bad for you."

"Yes, they are but these are better referred to as medications," Kiki explained, then bent a little towards her brother. "You know the other time you fell and had a little scratch, that ointment that was used on it is a medication, not a drug."

"Ohhh, I see," David said but still looked puzzled. "So what is the

difference between drugs and medications?"

"I don't think there is any difference, but we can ask Mom."

Just then, Mrs. Fash entered, wondering what the kids were busy with in grandma's room

"Mom, David thought Grandma was on drugs just because he saw her medication bag."

Mrs. Fash smiled and drew David closer in a warm embrace.

"Oh, no, my love. Grandma is on medication and not drugs like you mean it. When you say someone is on drugs, it means they have an addiction to certain drugs, especially those they are not supposed to be taking," Mrs. Fash tried to explain to her son.

"What is addiction?" David asked further.

"That is when people cannot do without doing something, even when it's harmful to them. An example is drug addiction, which is a form of drug abuse." Mrs. Fash added.

"Oh, so grandma is addicted to drugs since she cannot do without them?" David asked further and Kiki made a face at him.

Mrs. Fash came to David's rescue. "Not exactly, David. In grandma's case, her doctor wants her to keep using those medications, so she will not fall sick. But those who are addicted to drugs usually do not have their doctors' consent that it is okay to use the medication."

"Oh, I see!" David said. "So, with grandma, her doctor okays her using the drugs; that is why we call them medications and the other ones are kind of like using the drugs without their doctors saying it is okay?"

"Yes, my dear, and it can really have negative effects on their lives and behaviors. Sometimes they have to go to a special hospital called rehab to be able to stop it."

Mrs. Fash took a deep breath and continued: "So, grandma is not on drugs like those ones you think but using medications to help her health."

"Thank you, Mommy," David cooed. "I recall being taught that it is bad to be on drugs."

"Yes, David, it is bad to be on drugs, especially street drugs that turn people into addicts. But grandma is safe."

Mrs. Fash immediately began to think of how to secure the medications away from her children. She knew grandma must have mistakenly left the tablets on the table after taking her morning dose.

"Well, Mom, I am glad grandma is fine," David said, with a sober look. "I pray she will never be on drugs."

"Amen," Mrs. Fash said with a smile, and then added, "Drug, in that context, is bad and I pray for those who are addicted to get their healing and be free. May we be free from any addiction of any sort in Jesus' name."

"Amen," they all chorused.

Reflection

We must stay away from drugs and pills that have not be given to us by the doctors. They could be dangerous and deadly.

"All things are lawful for me, but all things are not helpful. All things are lawful for me, but I will not be brought under the power of any." (1 Corinthians 6:12)

6

UNTIMELY DEATH

It was a beautiful Saturday morning. David woke up so early and said his prayers. Since others were still asleep, he knew it would take some time before they had their family devotion. He rushed to brush his teeth, so he could play his favorite game; he was not in the mood for his piano this morning.

David loved Saturday mornings as there was no school and no one had to bother him to wake up to have his bath. This morning, he got so engrossed in his game and soon kept yelling, "Oh, I died!" Then, as he kept playing, he got excited as he won; but he was soon back to feeling sad and lamenting, "I died, I died!"

Mrs. Fash heard her little one yelling and jumped out of bed, wondering what was happening. Then, noticing that the noise was coming from the living room, she remembered that it was Saturday and knew it had to be a TV program or cartoon that David was watching. She opened the door to see her child and ensure he was safe.

"Good morning, Mom," David said, as he rushed to hug his mother. He was happy seeing a member of his family, especially his mom, this Saturday morning." "God bless you, David," Mrs. Fash said, as she bent down to hug her six-year-old. ."Why were you yelling "I died"? What are you watching?"

"It's a game, Mom, and I am a player in it." He pulled his mom to watch with him. She went along, curious to see what it was. She observed a game in which a player was running to avoid obstacles and enemies, and sometimes the player would be caught and killed. She did not like the game and asked her son to pause it for a moment.

"Oh, Mommy, why?" David whined. He had been so absorbed in the game.

"David," Mrs. Fash started, "I don't think I like a game that makes you feel you died."

"But, Mom, it's just a game," David protested further. "I died many times yesterday and two days ago but I'm still here."

Mrs. Fash shook her head, wondering where in the world she was when her son started playing this game.

"Where did you get this game from?"

"I got it from a friend at school, so I downloaded it to my tablet. But, Mom, no one truly dies; it's just a game!"

"I know," Mrs. Fash remarked. "But why a game of acting dead and not a game of you shining? No matter how it is presented, son, death is not a good thing for you, whether role-play or otherwise"

"Even in a game?" David asked innocently.

"Yes even in a game. You were so engrossed in the game you were yelling, "I died! I died!! David, do you not remember what I taught you about power in the tongue?" She paused for a moment to look at her son's face and see if he understood what she was saying. She recalled that they had the conversation recently.

David's face suddenly glowed in excitement. "Yes, I remember, Mommy, you said that we are what we say. So does that mean I can die by saying 'I die', 'I die'?"

"Well I pray for you that you will not die but live to declare the works of God but let's stay away from games and words around death."

"Mommy, I don't want to die."

"No, son, untimely death will not come near you, your siblings, or your parents, in Jesus' name."

"Amen," David replied and immediately added: "Mommy, please pray for me. I promise you not to play this game again. I think it is bad because it makes people die in the game."

Mrs. Fash nodded and held her son's hand.

"Father, Lord, we are thankful for life. We are also thankful for Your life in us. We come against any suggestions of death, be it in games and movies, or thoughts and words, or in any other form. We will not die but live to declare Your works. We pray against any spirit of untimely death over our family and over the body of Christ. In Jesus' name we pray."

"Amen," David said, and hugged his mom. He felt much better and relieved from the grip of the evil game. He promised himself never to play such a scary game again. His mother uninstall the game from his tablet.

Reflection

Death suggestions, no matter how subtle, must be dealt with. If it scares your child, it is important. Be careful of the apps, games and TV shows making death look okay. Be mindful, also, of the symbols of death on their clothing, shoes and other items, and avoid them. We must be vigilant and careful.

"Be sober, be vigilant; because your adversary the devil walks about like a roaring lion, seeking whom he may devour." (1 Peter 5:8).

7

SIBLING RIVALRY

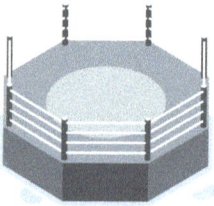

Kiki noticed that her classmate and friend, Shaunie, looked unhappy. She went over to her. "Is everything okay with you, Shaunie? You really look sad."

"It's my younger sister, Shauntel; my parents love her more than me," Shaunie muttered.

Kiki was a little startled and was initially unsure of how to respond. Her thoughts quickly flashed to her younger brother, David. Did her parents love him more than her? She remembered the many treats she had gotten and all the love she had received and decided in her heart that her parents loved her and her three brothers equally.

"I am so sorry to hear that," Kiki finally managed to say. "But your sister is such a nice girl like you. Why do you think your parents love her more?"

"They buy her more pretty dresses," Shaunie began. "And when they make her hair, they attach bows and flowers but don't do so for me. When I complain, they say it's because she is younger. I don't believe that because she is also a girl like me!"

Kiki hugged her friend and spoke kindly to her. "Shaunie, let's share this with Ms. Biggs," she suggested. Ms. Biggs was their class teacher and Kiki gently led Shaunie to her.

Ms. Biggs listened to Shaunie and Kiki. Then she spoke to Shaunie: "Do you think your dad and mom make enough time for you and Shauntel?"

Shaunie nodded, recalling the quality time her parents spend with them.

Just then, Ms. Biggs noticed something.

"Shaunie, I've just realized you are wearing a perm and you have a new flattened and very silky hair, while your sister has cornrows, which needed bows and flowers. Your hair just got done yesterday and your sister has been wearing hers for about a week now. So, it means your hair is newer and finer. Perhaps, the accessories added to Shauntel's hair are to make her feel she also has a new hair made."

A smile crept upon Shaunie's face, as she began to see the situation from a different angle. She nodded with excitement as she realized that she had truly just gotten her hair done.

"So, you see, I don't think your mom and dad love your sister more, but you can also discuss your concerns with them when you get home."

Shaunie felt much better and thanked Ms. Biggs. Then, she turned to Kiki and said, "Thank you, Kiki, for bringing me to Ms. Biggs. I feel better."

Kiki smiled back and hugged her. "You know, I think both you and Shauntel always look good for school," she said. "I think both of you are loved equally."

"True," Shaunie replied, "Ms. Biggs has just helped me to realize this."

"My mom once told me she loved me and my brothers equally and tries to show it."

"That's good, Kiki. Do you mind keeping me in your prayers so that my parents can keep loving Shauntel and me equally?"

"Yes, I will," Kiki assured. "We can even pray together right now."

"Okay."

"Father, I thank You for the life of Shaunie and her sister, Shauntel. I pray You continue to shower both of them with your unconditional love and care. Let each of them, especially, Shaunie, feel loved and cared for because You love us equally and died for us on the Cross. Thank you for loving Shaunie too and her sister. Help our parents to keep loving us equally, as you love us.

May your love continue to radiate over us, our siblings and our families in Jesus' name."

"Amen," Shaunie answered, feeling a reassuring wave of divine and parental love envelop her afresh.

Reflection

You are loved and cared for. Never allow anyone think your parents love your sibling more than you. You are perfect and different, so you are loved too.

"I will praise You, for I am fearfully and wonderfully made; Marvelous are Your works." (Psalm 139:14).

8

WORRY

David sat beside his dad in the living room, his head resting on his father's chest. Mr. Fash changed the channel to his favorite news channel. Just then, news of a plane crash came on. David became a little worried after this.

"Dad, did anyone survive the plane crash?" he asked.

"No, Son, unfortunately no one survived.

"Was Mommy on the plane?"

"Oh Lord, David, no! But why would you think of such a thing about your mom?"

David looked sober. "Because she has been travelling as a nurse and told me she flies a lot of planes."

"That's true," Mr. Fash said, "and we are thankful for journey mercies."

"Dad, can you please call mom, so I can speak to her?"

Mr. Fash glanced at the wall clock; it was a few minutes past nine. He guessed his wife would be busy on her night shift. She worked as a travel nurse at a big hospital in New York.

"Okay, David," Mr. Fash said. "I'll ring her once. She is most likely busy with her patients. If she doesn't pick then she will return our call when she has the time. I know you are worried because of the news but, trust me, your mom is safe, in Jesus' name."

"Amen."

Mr. Fash picked the cellphone and called his wife, turning on the speaker.

"Hello darling," came in Mrs. Fash's happy voice. David's face brightened immediately.

"David is worried about you because of a plane crash we just saw on the news."

"Oh, David, my darling," Mrs. Fash responded.

David took the phone from his dad.

"Mom," he gasped with joy. "I was super worried about you!"

"I know; your dad just told me. I am safe here in New York. Our God is watching over me, David."

"I love you, Mommy," David gushed. "I was just scared. You remember telling me you are always on the plane?"

"Yes, David, and God has always kept me."

"Yes, Mom. Can I pray for you, Mom?"

"Sure, David"

"Our heavenly Father. I thank you for Mom, who is safe in New York. I pray you always keep her safe. Mom, you will not have a plane crash or die but live to declare the works of the Lord. In Jesus' name I pray."

"Amen," chorused everyone.

Mrs. Fash was impressed. "David, thanks for being loving and caring," she said. "We also pray for those who have lost their loved ones through accidents that the Lord will comfort them. And for those of us always travelling or driving or even walking, our God will keep us safe, in Jesus' name. We pray against the spirit of worry and fear; we shall not be afraid of anyone or anything, in Jesus' name."

"Amen," they all said.

Reflection

All manner of worries brings anxiety and fear. It is important to commit your ways into the hands of God. When you commit your studies, family, and other things into the hands of God, He will take total control and give you peace of mind.

"The LORD is my light and my salvation; whom shall I fear? the LORD is the strength of my life; of whom shall I be afraid?" (Psalm 27:1).

9

OUR NATION

I t was the 4th of July, and David couldn't help but notice the American flags adorning every house in his neighborhood as he rode in his dad's car on the way to the grocery store.

"Dad," he asked, "why does every house have a flag today? Is it America's birthday?"

Mr. Fash smiled at his curious son. "Yes, David, it is! Remember, you don't have school today because it's a holiday?"

David nodded, and Mr. Fash decided to delve a bit deeper.

"What do you think of when you hear 'birthday,' David?"

David's face lit up with excitement. "Hmm, Daddy, I think of cupcakes, blowing out candles, gifts, friends, and toys!"

His dad chuckled. "Yes, that's usually what happens on birthdays. America got its independence from Great Britain on July 4th, 1776, and that's why today is celebrated as America's birthday."

As they got out of the car and headed towards the store, David's eyes widened with realization. "Wow, Dad, America is really old!"

"Well," Mr. Fash said with a wink, "let's just say America has many years of experience."

David pondered this for a moment before asking, "Is that why we sing the national anthem and say the pledge? Is the anthem like America's special birthday song?"

"The national anthem," Mr. Fash explained, holding David's hand, "reminds Americans of how hard they fought to be free. The pledge is a promise of loyalty and support to America."

"Awesome!" David exclaimed. "And Ms. Luke told us that the stars on the flag represent the fifty states of the United States."

"That's correct," Mr. Fash confirmed. "Can you name at least ten of them?"

"Sure, Daddy," David giggled. "Alabama, Alaska, Arizona, Arkansas, California, Colorado, Connecticut, Delaware, Florida, Georgia...and my favorite of all—TEXAS! I love the Cowboys!" Mr Fash laughed lightly.

As they approached the shopping carts, David eagerly pulled one out.

"Is Texas your favorite because you live here?" Mr. Fash asked with a smile.

"Yes, Daddy, and because I know you love the Cowboys," David chuckled, his excitement drawing warm smiles from passersby.

After a brief pause, David asked, "Daddy, where are we originally from?"

"Nigeria, my love. I was born and raised in Nigeria before moving to the States."

"Is that why we sometimes speak Yoruba at home?" David asked.

Mr. Fash smiled, appreciating his son's inquisitiveness. "Yes, we speak Yoruba, which is a language from the western part of Nigeria. Someday soon, we'll go on vacation to my hometown."

"I'd love to travel, Daddy. When is Nigeria's birthday?"

"October 1st."

"That's my birthday too!" David exclaimed.

"Yes, I know," Mr. Fash said with a smile. "You were born on Nigeria's Independence Day."

"Can we buy both flags here?" David asked eagerly.

"Of course, Mr. Prince," Mr. Fash replied, teasing him affectionately. David blushed and smiled back shyly.

At the store, David picked out both the American and Nigerian flags. Once they were back in the car, he eagerly suggested, "Dad, let's pray for America's birthday."

"Certainly," his father agreed.

Mr. Fash led the prayer: "Heavenly Father, thank You for the United States of America. Thank You for all the fifty states You created. Thank You for our president, lawmakers, and other government officials. We pray for Your peace in this land and for Your glory to shine. Give us hearts that love and serve You as a nation. We pray for everyone—young and old, white and black, male and female, of every tribe and background—that Your protection will be solid over us. Help us to be thankful for all You do and keep us as one nation under God, indivisible, in the name of Jesus, Your Son."

"Amen." David responded happily.

Reflection

Celebrating our nation's birthday is a special time for reflection and appreciation. Just as we value our personal birthdays, a nation's birthday is an opportunity to reflect on its history, progress, and the shared values that unite its people. It is also a time of sober reflection on what we have achieved versus what we could have achieved. As we grow older in age, a lot is expected of us in terms of our behaviors and habits. Birthdays are awesome. Let's enjoy the cake!

"All the ends of the world shall remember and turn to the Lord, *and all the families of the nations Shall worship before You. For the kingdom is the* Lord's, *And He rules over the nations."* (Psalm 22:27-28)

10

THOSE WHO DEFEND OUR NATION

It was Memorial Day, and the Fash family had extra time to sleep. David was the first to wake up. He wanted to eat some cake but remembered that he had been taught to always wait till after the morning prayers before having breakfast.

David went to the piano in the living room. He loved playing the piano; he attended piano lessons at his school every week. As he played, every member of the family began to wake up, one after the other. Isaiah and Elijah, his big brothers, came out of their room with their Bibles, as they knew it was time for the morning prayers. They walked tiredly to the living room. Kiki came out too and they met their mom, Mrs. Fash, in the living room already seated. Their maternal grandma was present, and they were singing, *"Good Morning Jesus, good morning Lord.»*

David left the piano, smiling. "Happy 4th of July," he said, excitedly.

"No, it's Memorial Day," Elijah corrected.

Mr. Fash came out of the room and was happy to see everyone ready for prayers and singing already. David indicated he wanted to lead the prayers today. He started: "Father we thank you for our family. Thank you for the United States of America. Thank you for our president, all our leaders and thank you for the State of Texas too, in Jesus name."

"Amen," everyone responded.

"Good job, David!" Mrs Fash cheered. "Now, let's pray a little more for this country."

Everyone closed their eyes again, as Mrs. Fash prayed: "Father, yes, we are indeed thankful for the USA. Thank You for the nation of our birth, too. Thank You for the leaders of this great country, thank You for the legislature, the executive and the judiciary. We thank You for all the parastatals and units. Thank You for the education sector and others – economic, health, housing, infrastructure, and so on. We pray that You keep us all safe and alive. We pray for every state, county and cities in the country, that Your presence will lead and guide their affairs, in Jesus' name."

"Amen," the family chorused.

"Mom, is it true I was born on Nigeria's birthday?" David asked.

"Yes you were born on October 1st, Nigeria's Independence Day."

"So, Nigeria's birthday is my birthday, even though I am an American?"

"Yes, Love," Grandma chipped in.

"I love the words, 'In God we trust', on our currency," Kiki said. Turning to grandma, she added, "Mom says it is a good thing to involve God in everything we do."

"That's true," Grandma affirmed with a smile.

"You saw the theme of our new home when we bought it, right?" Elijah asked.

"Dad named it 'Glory House'," Isaiah offered.

"And that is so cool," Kiki said. "I have never seen such in my friends' houses. Dad and Mom love to put God in everything."

"So does America," David offered, having heard *In God we trust* mentioned earlier.

"Well," said Mrs. Fash, "let's just say that the American dollar note has God's name on it. And remember that we also have 'one nation under God' in the Pledge of Allegiance. It is a beautiful thing for a nation to involve God in its affairs."

"Dad," David called, turning to Mr. Fash. "Did you know that the dollar note has 'In God we trust' on it?"

"Oh, really?" Mr Fash said, feigning surprise. "Who told you that?"

"Kiki says it is there on the currency and Mom and Elijah confirmed it."

"Awesome!"

"And our house has 'Glory House' written on it," David continued. "Can you please show me, Dad?"

"Alright, boy," Isaiah cut in, "let me show you." He took permission from his dad, then lifted David up and took him to the entrance of the house outside. Once there, he threw the already excited David up in the air twice, telling him to look out for the golden "Glory House" inscription.

"Did you see it?" he asked.

"Yes, I did!" David screamed happily.

When they got back inside, David announced to everyone that he had seen the special name. "When we have another house, we will put 'In God We Trust' on it," he added.

"Or 'One Home Under God, Indivisible," Kiki suggested.

"So, Dad, what is Memorial Day?" David asked

"It is a day set apart to remember men and women who died while serving in the US military. They left families behind - like wives, husbands and children. The day is used to honor their memories and sacrifices," Mr. Fash explained.

"We celebrate this the last Monday of May," Isaiah contributed.

"Oh, Dad, that is so scary," David observed. "Will you join the military too?"

"There is an age limit, David," Mr. Fash stated, giving David a reassuring smile. "Is that why you look so scared?"

"Not really, Dad. I was just concerned about those kids who lost their dads and moms."

"True," said Mr. Fash. "That is why a day like this exists and as your brother rightly said, it is a day set aside in their remembrance."

"Okay, Dad, can we pray for them too? And also, their families and loved ones."

"Okay, David, I will let you pray now."

David stood and prayed: "Father, we pray for all the families of those who died while serving our country that you provide food and toys for them. Bless the children and let them not die too. We also pray for those still serving that you protect them all, in Jesus' name."

Everyone smiled and said "Amen."

Reflection

Pray for the country of your origin and the country you are in now. Those who fought for freedom are precious and their memories are honored. Reflect on the soldiers and other personnel that fought hard for Independence, laying their lives down for our freedom.

"And we urge you, brethren, to recognize those who labor among you... to esteem them very highly in love for their work's sake..." (1 Thessalonians 5:12-13).

www.ingramcontent.com/pod-product-compliance
Lightning Source LLC
Chambersburg PA
CBHW041124120626
46547CB00019B/2836